BOYS
PASSWORD JOURNAL

Copyright 2014

Name/Company: _____

Website: _____

Email: _____

Username/Account: _____

Password: _____

Security Question: _____

Notes: _____

_____

Name/Company: _____

Website: _____

Email: _____

Username/Account: _____

Password: _____

Security Question: _____

Notes: _____

_____

Name/Company: _____

Website: _____

Email: _____

Username/Account: _____

Password: _____

Security Question: _____

Notes: _____

_____

Name/Company: _____

Website: _____

Email: _____

Username/Account: _____

Password: _____

Security Question: _____

Notes: _____

Name/Company: _____

Website: _____

Email: _____

Username/Account: _____

Password: _____

Security Question: _____

Notes: _____

_____

Name/Company: _____

Website: _____

Email: _____

Username/Account: _____

Password: _____

Security Question: _____

Notes: _____

_____

Name/Company: _____

Website: _____

Email: _____

Username/Account: _____

Password: _____

Security Question: _____

Notes: _____

_____

Name/Company: _____

Website: _____

Email: _____

Username/Account: _____

Password: _____

Security Question: _____

Notes: _____

Name/Company: _____

Website: _____

Email: _____

Username/Account: _____

Password: _____

Security Question: _____

Notes: _____

_____

Name/Company: _____

Website: _____

Email: _____

Username/Account: _____

Password: _____

Security Question: _____

Notes: _____

_____

Name/Company: _____

Website: _____

Email: _____

Username/Account: _____

Password: _____

Security Question: _____

Notes: _____

_____

Name/Company: _____

Website: _____

Email: _____

Username/Account: _____

Password: _____

Security Question: _____

Notes: _____

Name/Company: _____

Website: _____

Email: _____

Username/Account: _____

Password: _____

Security Question: _____

Notes: _____

_____

Name/Company: _____

Website: _____

Email: _____

Username/Account: _____

Password: _____

Security Question: _____

Notes: _____

_____

Name/Company: _____

Website: _____

Email: _____

Username/Account: _____

Password: _____

Security Question: _____

Notes: _____

_____

Name/Company: _____

Website: _____

Email: _____

Username/Account: _____

Password: _____

Security Question: _____

Notes: _____

Name/Company: _____

Website: _____

Email: _____

Username/Account: _____

Password: _____

Security Question: _____

Notes: _____

_____

Name/Company: _____

Website: _____

Email: _____

Username/Account: _____

Password: _____

Security Question: _____

Notes: _____

_____

Name/Company: _____

Website: _____

Email: _____

Username/Account: _____

Password: _____

Security Question: _____

Notes: _____

_____

Name/Company: _____

Website: _____

Email: _____

Username/Account: _____

Password: _____

Security Question: _____

Notes: _____

Name/Company: _____

Website: _____

Email: _____

Username/Account: _____

Password: _____

Security Question: _____

Notes: _____

_____

Name/Company: _____

Website: _____

Email: _____

Username/Account: _____

Password: _____

Security Question: _____

Notes: _____

_____

Name/Company: _____

Website: _____

Email: _____

Username/Account: _____

Password: _____

Security Question: _____

Notes: _____

_____

Name/Company: _____

Website: _____

Email: _____

Username/Account: _____

Password: _____

Security Question: _____

Notes: _____

Name/Company: _____

Website: _____

Email: _____

Username/Account: _____

Password: _____

Security Question: _____

Notes: _____

_____

Name/Company: _____

Website: _____

Email: _____

Username/Account: _____

Password: _____

Security Question: _____

Notes: _____

_____

Name/Company: _____

Website: _____

Email: _____

Username/Account: _____

Password: _____

Security Question: _____

Notes: _____

_____

Name/Company: _____

Website: _____

Email: _____

Username/Account: _____

Password: _____

Security Question: _____

Notes: _____

Name/Company: _____

Website: _____

Email: _____

Username/Account: _____

Password: _____

Security Question: _____

Notes: _____

_____

Name/Company: _____

Website: _____

Email: _____

Username/Account: _____

Password: _____

Security Question: _____

Notes: _____

_____

Name/Company: _____

Website: _____

Email: _____

Username/Account: _____

Password: _____

Security Question: _____

Notes: _____

_____

Name/Company: _____

Website: _____

Email: _____

Username/Account: _____

Password: _____

Security Question: _____

Notes: _____

Name/Company: _____

Website: _____

Email: _____

Username/Account: _____

Password: _____

Security Question: _____

Notes: _____

_____

Name/Company: _____

Website: _____

Email: _____

Username/Account: _____

Password: _____

Security Question: _____

Notes: _____

_____

Name/Company: _____

Website: _____

Email: _____

Username/Account: _____

Password: _____

Security Question: _____

Notes: _____

_____

Name/Company: _____

Website: _____

Email: _____

Username/Account: _____

Password: _____

Security Question: _____

Notes: _____

Name/Company: _____

Website: _____

Email: _____

Username/Account: _____

Password: _____

Security Question: _____

Notes: _____

_____

Name/Company: _____

Website: _____

Email: _____

Username/Account: _____

Password: _____

Security Question: _____

Notes: _____

_____

Name/Company: _____

Website: _____

Email: _____

Username/Account: _____

Password: _____

Security Question: _____

Notes: _____

_____

Name/Company: _____

Website: _____

Email: _____

Username/Account: _____

Password: _____

Security Question: _____

Notes: _____

Name/Company: _____

Website: _____

Email: _____

Username/Account: _____

Password: _____

Security Question: _____

Notes: _____

_____

Name/Company: _____

Website: _____

Email: _____

Username/Account: _____

Password: _____

Security Question: _____

Notes: _____

_____

Name/Company: _____

Website: _____

Email: _____

Username/Account: _____

Password: _____

Security Question: _____

Notes: _____

_____

Name/Company: _____

Website: _____

Email: _____

Username/Account: _____

Password: _____

Security Question: _____

Notes: _____

Name/Company: _____

Website: _____

Email: _____

Username/Account: _____

Password: _____

Security Question: _____

Notes: _____

_____

Name/Company: _____

Website: _____

Email: _____

Username/Account: _____

Password: _____

Security Question: _____

Notes: _____

_____

Name/Company: _____

Website: _____

Email: _____

Username/Account: _____

Password: _____

Security Question: _____

Notes: _____

_____

Name/Company: _____

Website: _____

Email: _____

Username/Account: _____

Password: _____

Security Question: _____

Notes: _____

Name/Company: _____

Website: _____

Email: _____

Username/Account: _____

Password: _____

Security Question: _____

Notes: _____

_____

Name/Company: _____

Website: _____

Email: _____

Username/Account: _____

Password: _____

Security Question: _____

Notes: _____

_____

Name/Company: _____

Website: _____

Email: _____

Username/Account: _____

Password: _____

Security Question: _____

Notes: _____

_____

Name/Company: _____

Website: _____

Email: _____

Username/Account: _____

Password: _____

Security Question: _____

Notes: _____

Name/Company: _____

Website: _____

Email: _____

Username/Account: _____

Password: _____

Security Question: _____

Notes: _____

_____

Name/Company: _____

Website: _____

Email: _____

Username/Account: _____

Password: _____

Security Question: _____

Notes: _____

_____

Name/Company: _____

Website: _____

Email: _____

Username/Account: _____

Password: _____

Security Question: _____

Notes: _____

_____

Name/Company: _____

Website: _____

Email: _____

Username/Account: _____

Password: _____

Security Question: _____

Notes: _____

Name/Company: _____

Website: _____

Email: _____

Username/Account: _____

Password: _____

Security Question: _____

Notes: _____

_____

Name/Company: _____

Website: _____

Email: _____

Username/Account: _____

Password: _____

Security Question: _____

Notes: _____

_____

Name/Company: _____

Website: _____

Email: _____

Username/Account: _____

Password: _____

Security Question: _____

Notes: _____

_____

Name/Company: _____

Website: _____

Email: _____

Username/Account: _____

Password: _____

Security Question: _____

Notes: _____

Name/Company: _____

Website: _____

Email: _____

Username/Account: _____

Password: _____

Security Question: _____

Notes: _____

_____

Name/Company: _____

Website: _____

Email: _____

Username/Account: _____

Password: _____

Security Question: _____

Notes: _____

_____

Name/Company: _____

Website: _____

Email: _____

Username/Account: _____

Password: _____

Security Question: _____

Notes: _____

_____

Name/Company: _____

Website: _____

Email: _____

Username/Account: _____

Password: _____

Security Question: _____

Notes: _____

Name/Company: _____

Website: _____

Email: _____

Username/Account: _____

Password: _____

Security Question: _____

Notes: _____

_____

Name/Company: _____

Website: _____

Email: _____

Username/Account: _____

Password: _____

Security Question: _____

Notes: _____

_____

Name/Company: _____

Website: _____

Email: _____

Username/Account: _____

Password: _____

Security Question: _____

Notes: _____

_____

Name/Company: _____

Website: _____

Email: _____

Username/Account: _____

Password: _____

Security Question: _____

Notes: _____

Name/Company: _____

Website: _____

Email: _____

Username/Account: _____

Password: _____

Security Question: _____

Notes: _____

_____

Name/Company: _____

Website: _____

Email: _____

Username/Account: _____

Password: _____

Security Question: _____

Notes: _____

_____

Name/Company: _____

Website: _____

Email: _____

Username/Account: _____

Password: _____

Security Question: _____

Notes: _____

_____

Name/Company: _____

Website: _____

Email: _____

Username/Account: _____

Password: _____

Security Question: _____

Notes: _____

Name/Company: _____

Website: _____

Email: _____

Username/Account: _____

Password: _____

Security Question: _____

Notes: _____

_____

Name/Company: _____

Website: _____

Email: _____

Username/Account: _____

Password: _____

Security Question: _____

Notes: _____

_____

Name/Company: _____

Website: _____

Email: _____

Username/Account: _____

Password: _____

Security Question: _____

Notes: _____

_____

Name/Company: _____

Website: _____

Email: _____

Username/Account: _____

Password: _____

Security Question: _____

Notes: _____

Name/Company: _____

Website: _____

Email: _____

Username/Account: _____

Password: _____

Security Question: _____

Notes: _____

_____

Name/Company: _____

Website: _____

Email: _____

Username/Account: _____

Password: _____

Security Question: _____

Notes: _____

_____

Name/Company: _____

Website: _____

Email: _____

Username/Account: _____

Password: _____

Security Question: _____

Notes: _____

_____

Name/Company: _____

Website: _____

Email: _____

Username/Account: _____

Password: _____

Security Question: _____

Notes: _____

Name/Company: _____

Website: _____

Email: _____

Username/Account: _____

Password: _____

Security Question: _____

Notes: _____

_____

Name/Company: _____

Website: _____

Email: _____

Username/Account: _____

Password: _____

Security Question: _____

Notes: _____

_____

Name/Company: _____

Website: _____

Email: _____

Username/Account: _____

Password: _____

Security Question: _____

Notes: _____

_____

Name/Company: _____

Website: _____

Email: _____

Username/Account: _____

Password: _____

Security Question: _____

Notes: _____

Name/Company: _____

Website: _____

Email: _____

Username/Account: _____

Password: _____

Security Question: _____

Notes: _____

_____

Name/Company: _____

Website: _____

Email: _____

Username/Account: _____

Password: _____

Security Question: _____

Notes: _____

_____

Name/Company: _____

Website: _____

Email: _____

Username/Account: _____

Password: _____

Security Question: _____

Notes: _____

_____

Name/Company: _____

Website: _____

Email: _____

Username/Account: _____

Password: _____

Security Question: _____

Notes: _____

Name/Company: _____

Website: _____

Email: _____

Username/Account: _____

Password: _____

Security Question: _____

Notes: _____

_____

Name/Company: _____

Website: _____

Email: _____

Username/Account: _____

Password: _____

Security Question: _____

Notes: _____

_____

Name/Company: _____

Website: _____

Email: _____

Username/Account: _____

Password: _____

Security Question: _____

Notes: _____

_____

Name/Company: _____

Website: _____

Email: _____

Username/Account: _____

Password: _____

Security Question: _____

Notes: _____

Name/Company: _____

Website: _____

Email: _____

Username/Account: _____

Password: _____

Security Question: _____

Notes: _____

_____

Name/Company: _____

Website: _____

Email: _____

Username/Account: _____

Password: _____

Security Question: _____

Notes: _____

_____

Name/Company: _____

Website: _____

Email: _____

Username/Account: _____

Password: _____

Security Question: _____

Notes: _____

_____

Name/Company: _____

Website: _____

Email: _____

Username/Account: _____

Password: _____

Security Question: _____

Notes: _____

Name/Company: _____

Website: _____

Email: _____

Username/Account: _____

Password: _____

Security Question: _____

Notes: _____

_____

Name/Company: _____

Website: _____

Email: _____

Username/Account: _____

Password: _____

Security Question: _____

Notes: _____

_____

Name/Company: _____

Website: _____

Email: _____

Username/Account: _____

Password: _____

Security Question: _____

Notes: _____

_____

Name/Company: _____

Website: _____

Email: _____

Username/Account: _____

Password: _____

Security Question: _____

Notes: _____

Name/Company: _____

Website: _____

Email: _____

Username/Account: _____

Password: _____

Security Question: _____

Notes: _____

_____

Name/Company: _____

Website: _____

Email: _____

Username/Account: _____

Password: _____

Security Question: _____

Notes: _____

_____

Name/Company: _____

Website: _____

Email: _____

Username/Account: _____

Password: _____

Security Question: _____

Notes: _____

_____

Name/Company: _____

Website: _____

Email: _____

Username/Account: _____

Password: _____

Security Question: _____

Notes: _____

Name/Company: _____

Website: _____

Email: _____

Username/Account: _____

Password: _____

Security Question: _____

Notes: _____

_____

Name/Company: _____

Website: _____

Email: _____

Username/Account: _____

Password: _____

Security Question: _____

Notes: _____

_____

Name/Company: _____

Website: _____

Email: _____

Username/Account: _____

Password: _____

Security Question: _____

Notes: _____

_____

Name/Company: _____

Website: _____

Email: _____

Username/Account: _____

Password: _____

Security Question: _____

Notes: _____

Name/Company: _____

Website: _____

Email: _____

Username/Account: _____

Password: _____

Security Question: _____

Notes: _____

_____

Name/Company: _____

Website: _____

Email: _____

Username/Account: _____

Password: _____

Security Question: _____

Notes: _____

_____

Name/Company: _____

Website: _____

Email: _____

Username/Account: _____

Password: _____

Security Question: _____

Notes: _____

_____

Name/Company: _____

Website: _____

Email: _____

Username/Account: _____

Password: _____

Security Question: _____

Notes: _____

Name/Company: _____

Website: _____

Email: _____

Username/Account: _____

Password: _____

Security Question: _____

Notes: _____

_____

Name/Company: _____

Website: _____

Email: _____

Username/Account: _____

Password: _____

Security Question: _____

Notes: _____

_____

Name/Company: _____

Website: _____

Email: _____

Username/Account: _____

Password: _____

Security Question: _____

Notes: _____

_____

Name/Company: _____

Website: _____

Email: _____

Username/Account: _____

Password: _____

Security Question: _____

Notes: _____

Name/Company: _____

Website: _____

Email: _____

Username/Account: _____

Password: _____

Security Question: _____

Notes: _____

_____

Name/Company: _____

Website: _____

Email: _____

Username/Account: _____

Password: _____

Security Question: _____

Notes: _____

_____

Name/Company: _____

Website: _____

Email: _____

Username/Account: _____

Password: _____

Security Question: _____

Notes: _____

_____

Name/Company: _____

Website: _____

Email: _____

Username/Account: _____

Password: _____

Security Question: _____

Notes: _____

Name/Company: _____

Website: _____

Email: _____

Username/Account: _____

Password: _____

Security Question: _____

Notes: _____

_____

Name/Company: _____

Website: _____

Email: _____

Username/Account: _____

Password: _____

Security Question: _____

Notes: _____

_____

Name/Company: _____

Website: _____

Email: _____

Username/Account: _____

Password: _____

Security Question: _____

Notes: _____

_____

Name/Company: _____

Website: _____

Email: _____

Username/Account: _____

Password: _____

Security Question: _____

Notes: _____

Name/Company: _____

Website: _____

Email: _____

Username/Account: _____

Password: _____

Security Question: _____

Notes: _____

_____

Name/Company: _____

Website: _____

Email: _____

Username/Account: _____

Password: _____

Security Question: _____

Notes: _____

_____

Name/Company: _____

Website: _____

Email: _____

Username/Account: _____

Password: _____

Security Question: _____

Notes: _____

_____

Name/Company: _____

Website: _____

Email: _____

Username/Account: _____

Password: _____

Security Question: _____

Notes: _____

Name/Company: _____

Website: _____

Email: _____

Username/Account: _____

Password: _____

Security Question: _____

Notes: _____

_____

Name/Company: _____

Website: _____

Email: _____

Username/Account: _____

Password: _____

Security Question: _____

Notes: _____

_____

Name/Company: _____

Website: _____

Email: _____

Username/Account: _____

Password: _____

Security Question: _____

Notes: _____

_____

Name/Company: _____

Website: _____

Email: _____

Username/Account: _____

Password: _____

Security Question: _____

Notes: _____

Name/Company: _____

Website: _____

Email: _____

Username/Account: _____

Password: _____

Security Question: _____

Notes: _____

_____

Name/Company: _____

Website: _____

Email: _____

Username/Account: _____

Password: _____

Security Question: _____

Notes: _____

_____

Name/Company: _____

Website: _____

Email: _____

Username/Account: _____

Password: _____

Security Question: _____

Notes: _____

_____

Name/Company: _____

Website: _____

Email: _____

Username/Account: _____

Password: _____

Security Question: _____

Notes: _____

Name/Company: _____

Website: _____

Email: _____

Username/Account: _____

Password: _____

Security Question: _____

Notes: _____

_____

Name/Company: _____

Website: _____

Email: _____

Username/Account: _____

Password: _____

Security Question: _____

Notes: _____

_____

Name/Company: _____

Website: _____

Email: _____

Username/Account: _____

Password: _____

Security Question: _____

Notes: _____

_____

Name/Company: _____

Website: _____

Email: _____

Username/Account: _____

Password: _____

Security Question: _____

Notes: _____

Name/Company: _____

Website: _____

Email: _____

Username/Account: _____

Password: _____

Security Question: _____

Notes: _____

_____

Name/Company: _____

Website: _____

Email: _____

Username/Account: _____

Password: _____

Security Question: _____

Notes: _____

_____

Name/Company: _____

Website: _____

Email: _____

Username/Account: _____

Password: _____

Security Question: _____

Notes: _____

_____

Name/Company: _____

Website: _____

Email: _____

Username/Account: _____

Password: _____

Security Question: _____

Notes: _____

Name/Company: _____

Website: _____

Email: _____

Username/Account: _____

Password: _____

Security Question: _____

Notes: _____

_____

Name/Company: _____

Website: _____

Email: _____

Username/Account: _____

Password: _____

Security Question: _____

Notes: _____

_____

Name/Company: _____

Website: _____

Email: _____

Username/Account: _____

Password: _____

Security Question: _____

Notes: _____

_____

Name/Company: _____

Website: _____

Email: _____

Username/Account: _____

Password: _____

Security Question: _____

Notes: _____

Name/Company: _____

Website: _____

Email: _____

Username/Account: _____

Password: _____

Security Question: _____

Notes: _____

_____

Name/Company: _____

Website: _____

Email: _____

Username/Account: _____

Password: _____

Security Question: _____

Notes: _____

_____

Name/Company: _____

Website: _____

Email: _____

Username/Account: _____

Password: _____

Security Question: _____

Notes: _____

_____

Name/Company: _____

Website: _____

Email: _____

Username/Account: _____

Password: _____

Security Question: _____

Notes: _____

Name/Company: _____

Website: _____

Email: _____

Username/Account: _____

Password: _____

Security Question: _____

Notes: _____

_____

Name/Company: _____

Website: _____

Email: _____

Username/Account: _____

Password: _____

Security Question: _____

Notes: _____

_____

Name/Company: _____

Website: _____

Email: _____

Username/Account: _____

Password: _____

Security Question: _____

Notes: _____

_____

Name/Company: _____

Website: _____

Email: _____

Username/Account: _____

Password: _____

Security Question: _____

Notes: _____

Name/Company: _____

Website: _____

Email: _____

Username/Account: _____

Password: _____

Security Question: _____

Notes: _____

_____

Name/Company: _____

Website: _____

Email: _____

Username/Account: _____

Password: _____

Security Question: _____

Notes: _____

_____

Name/Company: _____

Website: _____

Email: _____

Username/Account: _____

Password: _____

Security Question: _____

Notes: _____

_____

Name/Company: _____

Website: _____

Email: _____

Username/Account: _____

Password: _____

Security Question: _____

Notes: _____

Name/Company: _____

Website: _____

Email: _____

Username/Account: _____

Password: _____

Security Question: _____

Notes: _____

_____

Name/Company: _____

Website: _____

Email: _____

Username/Account: _____

Password: _____

Security Question: _____

Notes: _____

_____

Name/Company: _____

Website: _____

Email: _____

Username/Account: _____

Password: _____

Security Question: _____

Notes: _____

_____

Name/Company: _____

Website: _____

Email: _____

Username/Account: _____

Password: _____

Security Question: _____

Notes: _____

Name/Company: _____

Website: _____

Email: _____

Username/Account: _____

Password: _____

Security Question: _____

Notes: _____
_____

Name/Company: _____

Website: _____

Email: _____

Username/Account: _____

Password: _____

Security Question: _____

Notes: _____
_____

Name/Company: _____

Website: _____

Email: _____

Username/Account: _____

Password: _____

Security Question: _____

Notes: _____
_____

Name/Company: _____

Website: _____

Email: _____

Username/Account: _____

Password: _____

Security Question: _____

Notes: _____

Name/Company: _____

Website: _____

Email: _____

Username/Account: _____

Password: _____

Security Question: _____

Notes: _____

_____

Name/Company: _____

Website: _____

Email: _____

Username/Account: _____

Password: _____

Security Question: _____

Notes: _____

_____

Name/Company: _____

Website: _____

Email: _____

Username/Account: _____

Password: _____

Security Question: _____

Notes: _____

_____

Name/Company: _____

Website: _____

Email: _____

Username/Account: _____

Password: _____

Security Question: _____

Notes: _____

Name/Company: _____

Website: _____

Email: _____

Username/Account: _____

Password: _____

Security Question: _____

Notes: _____

_____

Name/Company: _____

Website: _____

Email: _____

Username/Account: _____

Password: _____

Security Question: _____

Notes: _____

_____

Name/Company: _____

Website: _____

Email: _____

Username/Account: _____

Password: _____

Security Question: _____

Notes: _____

_____

Name/Company: _____

Website: _____

Email: _____

Username/Account: _____

Password: _____

Security Question: _____

Notes: _____

Name/Company: _____

Website: _____

Email: _____

Username/Account: _____

Password: _____

Security Question: _____

Notes: _____

_____

Name/Company: _____

Website: _____

Email: _____

Username/Account: _____

Password: _____

Security Question: _____

Notes: _____

_____

Name/Company: _____

Website: _____

Email: _____

Username/Account: _____

Password: _____

Security Question: _____

Notes: _____

_____

Name/Company: _____

Website: _____

Email: _____

Username/Account: _____

Password: _____

Security Question: _____

Notes: _____

Name/Company: _____

Website: _____

Email: _____

Username/Account: _____

Password: _____

Security Question: _____

Notes: _____
_____

Name/Company: _____

Website: _____

Email: _____

Username/Account: _____

Password: _____

Security Question: _____

Notes: _____
_____

Name/Company: _____

Website: _____

Email: _____

Username/Account: _____

Password: _____

Security Question: _____

Notes: _____
_____

Name/Company: _____

Website: _____

Email: _____

Username/Account: _____

Password: _____

Security Question: _____

Notes: _____

Name/Company: _____

Website: _____

Email: _____

Username/Account: _____

Password: _____

Security Question: _____

Notes: _____

_____

Name/Company: _____

Website: _____

Email: _____

Username/Account: _____

Password: _____

Security Question: _____

Notes: _____

_____

Name/Company: _____

Website: _____

Email: _____

Username/Account: _____

Password: _____

Security Question: _____

Notes: _____

_____

Name/Company: _____

Website: _____

Email: _____

Username/Account: _____

Password: _____

Security Question: _____

Notes: _____

Name/Company: _____

Website: _____

Email: _____

Username/Account: _____

Password: _____

Security Question: _____

Notes: _____

_____

Name/Company: _____

Website: _____

Email: _____

Username/Account: _____

Password: _____

Security Question: _____

Notes: _____

_____

Name/Company: _____

Website: _____

Email: _____

Username/Account: _____

Password: _____

Security Question: _____

Notes: _____

_____

Name/Company: _____

Website: _____

Email: _____

Username/Account: _____

Password: _____

Security Question: _____

Notes: _____